I Am
Michelle Obama:
The First Lady

by
Margina Graham Parker

Illustrations by
Marco Birge

ISBN 978-0-9841829-0-9
Library of Congress Control Number: 2009934474

Tumaini Publishing, Inc
3939 Lavista Road Suite E 360
Tucker, GA 30084
www.tumainipublishing.com

"Look at me in my pretty dress, my shoes are just right, my hat's the best!

I'm all dressed up, for the world to see,
I'm Michelle Obama, The First Lady."

"Absolutely dear, whatever you want, you can be.
But I must tell you more about our First Lady.

You see there's much more to her than just clothes and fashion. She's an accomplished woman, helping people, that's her passion."

"Mommy, tell me more, I want to know everything!"
"Just wait honey, I'll tell you, but we must start at the begin-ning.

The Southside of Chicago is where she got her start.
And to this day, the city still remains in her heart.

Michelle was raised by both her mom and dad.
In a one room apartment, with her brother, Craig.

She excelled in school, good marks were all she made. She was such a great student, That she skipped the second grade!

Michelle kept up her grades, through elementary and middle school she passed. And when she graduated high school, she finished second in her class!

She continued onto college, focused on her ambition.
In 1985, she graduated with honors,
From a university named Princeton.

Michelle attended law school at Harvard,
always reaching for the top.
While working for a prestigious law firm,
she met a young man named, Barack.

They soon fell in love,
she had changed his life.
After dating several years,
he asked her to become his wife.

Michelle fulfilled her dream,
by becoming a mother.
Malia, was her first child,
but soon came another.

Natasha, is what they named,
their second daughter.
These girls are indeed blessed
with a great mother and father.

But being a mom,
was just one title of many.
Michelle was the
Vice-President at a hospital, and
a dean at Chicago University."

"But Mommy, wasn't Mrs.
Obama also a lawyer?"
"That's true, she was,
and in Chicago, she even
worked for the mayor.

She was also a community leader, helping those who didn't have a voice.
Empowering the people is what mattered to her, letting them know that they have a choice."

"But Mommy, how did she manage?
It sounds like she was busy!"
"That may have been the case, sweetheart,
but that's what makes her such a great lady.

When her husband, Barack, decided that he, wanted to be President of the United States, Michelle was as happy as could be!

From that moment on, Michelle and Barack were on a mission,
they spoke of Hope and of Change,
to anyone that would listen.

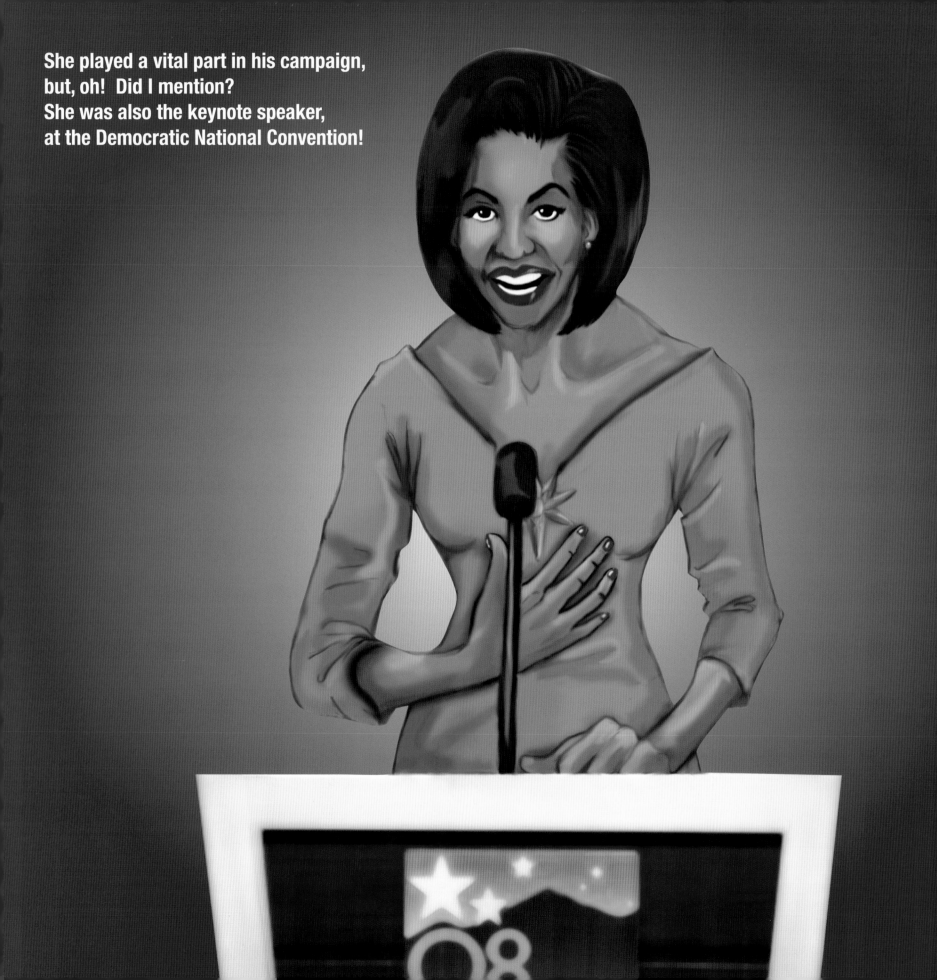

But even while being the First Lady with all it's fame, Mrs. Obama still finds the time to do fun things, like play Monopoly® and other board games.

Now here's the part,
that interests you best.
Mrs. Obama is now a fashion icon,
that means she really can dress.

Everyone wants to see, what it is that she wears, people "ooh" and "ahh", they point and stare.

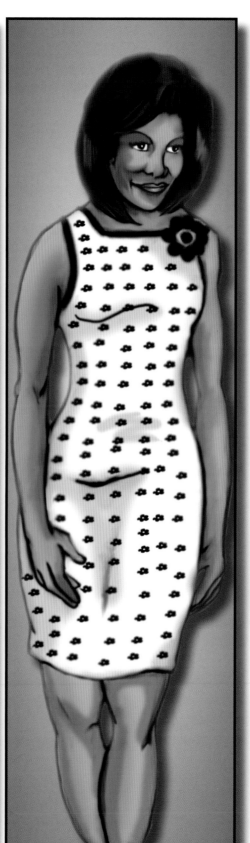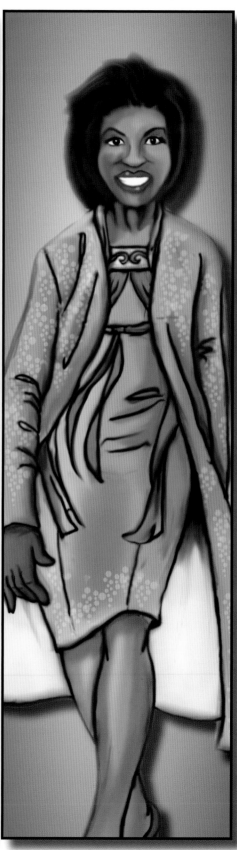

"Mommy, I think it's nice,
that she dresses so well,
but now I know her story,
and there's so much more to tell.

Michelle Obama is our First Lady
and she has a big job to do.
But even more what's important,
is that she's a great mommy,
just like you!"

Michelle LaVaughn Robinson Obama

First Lady of the United States of America

"And although the circumstances of our lives may seem very distant, with me standing here as the First Lady of the United States of America, I want you to know that we have very much in common, for nothing in my life's path would of predicted that I would be standing here as the First African-American, First Lady of the United States of America. There was nothing in my story that would land me here. I wasn't raised with wealth or resources or any social standing to speak of, I was raised on the Southside of Chicago. And my brother and I was raised with all that you really need, love, strong values and a believe that with a good education and a whole lot of hard work, that there was nothing that we could not do. If you want to know the reason why I'm standing here, it's because of education, and by getting a good education you too can control your own destiny."

Important Dates

🗝️ January 17, 1964 - Michelle LaVaughn Robinson is born in Chicago, Illinois

🗝️ 1981 - Graduates from Whitney Young High School as saluatorian

🗝️ 1985 - Graduates from Princeton University

🗝️ 1988 - Graduates from Harvard Law School ; begins working at Sidley-Austin law firm

🗝️ 1989 - Begins working with Barack Obama as his mentor

🗝️ July 1991 - Begins working for the mayor of Chicago, Richard Daley

🗝️ October 18, 1992 - Marries Barack Obama at Trinity United Church of Christ in Chicago

🗝️ July 4, 1998 - Gives birth to Malia Ann

🗝️ June 10, 2001 - Give birth to Natasha (Sasha)

🗝️ 2002 - Named Director of Community Affairs at the University of Chicago Hospitals

🗝️ August 25, 2008 - Delivers the keynote address at the Democratic National Convention in Denver, Colorado

🗝️ November 4, 2008 - Husband Barack Obama is elected as the 44th President of the United States of America